MW00955422

ALICE THE ACE

From We Can't to We Can Series

Author and Illustrator: Trinity Jagdeo
Editor: Evan Morris

Copyright © 2018 by Trinity Jagdeo
All rights reserved.
ISBN: 1727577132
ISBN-13: 978-1727577136

About the author and illustrator:

Trinity Jagdeo is a motivated teenager who aspires to change society for the better through books and community outreach.

About the editor:

Evan Morris is a bright teenager who, through hard work and determination, hopes to improve the world's outlook on those with disabilities.

Inspired by the many children that live with a little extra piece to them.

The Adventures of
Alice the Ace!

"Do you think that you can reach the next bar?" asked Dad. "Be strong and courageous!"

"I think...I think I can! I can do anything!" Alice replied.

"Fantastic job Alice! Let's take a break. I will be sitting on the green bench, remember that, okay Alice?" explained Dad.

"Okay. Green bench. Got it," Alice remarked.

"My dad is helpful; I need his help.
I'm a little different, but that makes
him love me even more!"
Alice explained.

"Wait a minute, I think I hear someone that needs help. It's time to be..."

"ALICE THE ACE"

"Look closely, I see a kitten
stuck in a tree! Oh, no!"
cried Alice.

"Here, kitty, kitty, kitty! Don't be scared, Alice the Ace is here to help!"
called Alice.

"But, how can I get her down?" wondered Alice.

"I know, I can use my special art pad to create a..."

"...ladder! I'll draw one ladder
with 4 rungs just to be safe,"
announced Alice.

"I feel a little scared, but I need to be strong and courageous!" declared Alice.

"Here kitty, I have you!"

"Where is your family? I don't
see anyone."

"I will use my hearing sense!
There! That boy is searching
for something!" stated Alice.

"I am feeling shy, but I know
I need to be strong."

"Is this your kitten? She was stuck in a tree," remarked Alice.

"Yes! Oh, Claire, I have been looking for you silly kitty! Thank you! You are so brave!" Zayn exclaimed.

"Now it's time to find Dad.
Where is he?" Alice wondered.

"Oh, right, the green bench!"

"Alice! You found me, great job! How are you feeling?" asked Dad.

"I feel happy, Dad! Thank you for bringing me here today," Alice cheered.

"You played well today. Let's go get ice cream," Dad said with excitement.

Deuteronomy 31:6-
"Be strong and courageous. Do not be afraid or terrified because of them, for the Lord your God goes with you; he will never leave you nor forsake you."

Visit us at www.wecant2wecan.org
And find our social media pages @wecant2wecan

Made in the USA
Coppell, TX
03 January 2021

47484738R00019